Praise for *Sorting Out Behaviour*

I strongly recommend this extremely useful and practical guide, which demonstrates that effective behaviour management is about clarity, transparency, consistency and a set of manageable policies and procedures which are kept under constant review. Drawing on the author's vast, first-hand experience, it is a source of common sense and practical pointers which would enable all school staff from trainees to experienced school leaders to review their behaviour policies, practices and procedures.

Brian Lightman, General Secretary, Association of School and College Leaders

Thank you to Jeremy Rowe for providing a plain English, common sense, easy to read guide about behaviour. Perhaps more importantly, he reminds us that children aren't criminals and that most schools are calm, productive, orderly places that are far removed from the image so often portrayed in the media. We need to hear that message more often.

Fiona Millar, Guardian Columnist

SORTING OUT
BEHAVIOUR

SORTING OUT BEHAVIOUR

A head teacher's guide

Jeremy Rowe

First published by
Independent Thinking Press
Crown Buildings, Bancyfelin, Carmarthen, Wales, SA33 5ND, UK
www.independentthinkingpress.com

Independent Thinking Press is an imprint of Crown House Publishing Ltd.

© Jeremy Rowe 2013

Illustrations © Les Evans 2013

Image cover, title page and page 90 © adore, Fotolia.com

British Library Cataloguing-in-Publication Data
A catalogue entry for this book is available
from the British Library.

Print ISBN 978-1-78135-011-9
Mobi ISBN 978-1-78135-033-1
ePub ISBN 978-1-78135-034-8

Printed and bound in the UK by
Gomer Press, Llandysul, Ceredigion

This book is dedicated to the hundreds of thousands of children who, despite leading difficult lives, come to our schools every day in a spirit of generosity and hope. It is an honour and a privilege to have the chance to build schools in which these fantastic children can soar, become great and leave their trace across the sky.

And to Harriet, of course, with love.

Contents

Introduction

Like most of us, I've worked in schools that have got their approach to behaviour right and in some that have got it wrong. Right is better. I've been lucky to have had the opportunity to work with magnificent teams at Pool Academy in Cornwall and Sir John Leman High School in Suffolk, both of which are packed with colleagues who know it is possible to improve and have been prepared to do what is needed to make that improvement happen.

By working together consistently and strategically, both schools were able to see genuine improvements. This can only be achieved by teams unswervingly operating value-based systems. Without that, staff are out on a limb and the minority of students who can be difficult will have a field day.

Like you, I am doing the job day-in and day-out and, like you, I get it wrong sometimes. In fact, the minute you think you've sussed it, a child will literally take your legs from under you! Remembering that is quite helpful, I think.

My basic view is that behaviour is about choice. That doesn't mean that situations are equally easy for all of us to handle, but I believe that if we factor choice out of a situation we could be robbing an individual of their entitlements and their independence. If we were all predestined to behave in certain ways, all responses would be predictable. People choose how they behave. All of us.

Below is a short quiz:

Can bad behaviour be eradicated in our schools?

Can it be improved?

Should we try to improve it?*

For me, everything became clear as a result of one early conversation I had in which I was told there was no soap in the students' toilets because 'they messed around with it'. What this meant was that a couple of students did. What it really meant, though, was both profound and frightening. It did not simply mean that one or two students were running the school. They had in fact, been given the power to do something much more important. They were being allowed to *define* the school. No child could wash their hands because one or two students didn't want them to. From that point onwards, I made a virtue out of taking risks with what students could 'cope with' – and never looked back.

I hope that this book provides a straightforward description of what we do, and why we feel these approaches work. None of the ideas are patented; all of them are taken wholesale or adapted from other schools. You will know the idiosyncrasies of your own school and what would be successful.

---

*Answers: No, Yes, Yes.

I'm not using a Marxist or feminist perspective – mainly because I don't understand them. I haven't done a lot of research either, because I was too busy actually improving our school – so there aren't twenty pages of references at the back. Sorry.

Incidentally, it is important to remember that children are not criminals and that the negative behavioural choices a minority occasionally make are not crimes. Our job isn't about retribution; it is about ensuring young people learn from their mistakes, so they can take their place in society and succeed.

My intention is to set out a simple, occasionally slightly difficult, approach to student behaviour that actually works. My school isn't perfect, but it is better as a result. And that's important.

Key points

- All schools can be made even better
- The outcome is worth it
- The students are worth it

Sorting out mistakes

It is currently very popular to talk about how great mistakes are – as in, you can only learn by making mistakes. While I've no doubt there is a lot of truth in this, I still think that mistakes are overrated. What's wrong with learning by getting it right first time?

Tackling behavioural issues requires a lot of thinking, planning and consistent delivery. Errors will make you look ridiculous, will make people question the rigour of your planning and will undermine your efforts, confidence and credibility. They are probably best avoided.

I've read that one supermarket chain is so successful because they 'keep it very simple, and they execute brilliantly'. Sounds good to me (unless they are doing actual executions, which a good approach to behavioural management should try to avoid).

Sorting out assemblies

Assemblies are one of the many great ways that you can use to show you mean business in a school. I'm not talking about a thundering, red-faced tirade from the lectern, though. Well-organised assemblies, with form tutors lining the sides to keep an eye on things, send out a subliminal message about your school: in this case, that it is a disciplined and well-controlled environment. There is nothing wrong with that – many of your students are crying out for the chance to thrive within a bit of structure and order.

Students entering in silence is important: if you don't feel you can achieve it yet, stick it on your behavioural timeline (see page 70) for next term, from September with the new year group or whenever you feel you can achieve it by. 'Yet' is a great word – as in 'we haven't tackled that, yet'.

Of course, great assemblies are also a fantastic platform to celebrate success. Sometimes you will need to train children to be able to give and receive praise properly. I saw this done incredibly well by the wonderful students at Robert Clack School in Dagenham while sitting next to the inspirational Sir Paul Grant. Student after student stood up to receive the applause of their peers for their accomplishments. It was amazing and an excellent example of what great leadership and high expectations can achieve.

Key points

- Assemblies should focus on positives
- They should be interesting and well organised
- Students should enter in silence – this is very powerful

Sorting out the
primary/secondary thing

We all know it is easy to get distracted away from the primary problem but still often forget, especially in the heat of the moment. It is best clarified by an example: you ask a student for their hat, they tell you they would prefer not to give it to you and back this up with a few swear words. Our instinctive approach is to immediately focus on the swearing – which, let's be honest, is more serious. But that is not the point: whatever sanction you give, unless you *still* get the hat, the young person will conclude that they have won that encounter because they did not hand over the hat. And in a sense, they'd be right.

The good news is that when you deal with the primary problem first – and this can be difficult as well as counter-intuitive – then dealing with the secondary issue – which could well be more serious – will be much easier.

Children, and even occasionally parents, will often throw something in – like swearing – to divert you away from the original conversation. At our school we always get the hat, phone or whatever. Even if we have to wait; there is no way that child is going back into lessons until it has been done, regardless of what sanctions were applied for the secondary action. Is this petty? I don't think so. If it is, it shouldn't have been an issue in the first place.

Sorting out being present

Eighty percent of success is showing up.

Woody Allen

It is essential you are out there – for members of the senior team, and even more so for head teachers, to have a visible presence around the school. You cannot lead your school by emails or memos. You need to walk it and feel it, talk to people and watch people. Every day. However, there is other work to be done too. So how do you balance competing demands for your time?

The answer for me has been to plan the time I spend around the school in order to maximise its impact. The following combination will give you a good presence:

- Standing at strategic points during lesson changeovers
- Being at the entrance and exit at the start and end of the school day
- Popping into each classroom at least once a week

Sorting out a Hall of Fame

Big pictures, nicely framed, of our students doing fantastic things. That's it. Impact? Phenomenal.

Sorting out consistency

Just asking a child to put something away, or to promise not to wear a banned item again, is not really a good idea. If they promise to put the hat away for the rest of the day, they might. Then again, they may wear it into the next lesson and tell the teacher that the previous teacher had allowed them to do so. The second teacher then becomes resentful of the first teacher and, in that case, decides they won't confiscate the hat either. Poor old teacher number three does what she is supposed to and asks for the hat. To the student she now seems unreasonable. In a sense, she is. The hypocrisy of her colleagues has undermined her and the school's values and left her in a far more difficult situation.

It's all about consistency. You're swimming against the tide without it.

Sorting out the tracking of behaviour

To go into a classroom and let a student – and their peers – know that you are disappointed that they have received a consequence during that lesson is literally amazing. Teachers appreciate it because it says, loud and clear, that we are all working together and that we are all intolerant of anything which gets in the way of our learning. It is essential to do the same for a positive consequence, of course, of which there should be vastly more.

So how do we do this? My system is very simple. Students can get a credit from their teacher, which is stored in their personal account and regularly cashed in for prizes. Conversely, before a detention they are given two formal warnings (C1, C2) which are also recorded. An actual detention is recorded as a C3 and is *always* served.

At meetings with parents, it is very helpful to be able to call on this information. Whatever computer management system your school uses, there will be a way for teachers to do this, and for pastoral and senior staff to monitor it in real time.

At the time of writing, I can tell you how many credits were awarded and how many warnings were given, to whom, and why, across the whole school. This means that, over time, we can see if there is a problem with a particular teacher, subject, gender, group of students, time of day, part of the school and so on, and deal with it. It's brilliant.

Key points

■ Pick the right management system

■ Use it in a way that most benefits your school

■ Ensure teachers are being consistent and fair

■ Watch the number of negative consequences fall and the positives rise

Sorting out the school's reaction to change

I can guarantee the response to any changes you bring in which are designed to raise standards, from sorting out short skirts to tackling attendance. It will be something like this:

A. **Launch**

Everyone involved, high motivation and confidence. Lovely, basically.

B. **First few hours/days**

Suddenly this is looking difficult – the problems are actually going up. Doubt is starting to creep in.

C. **Not long after this**

A few loyal followers have melted away. The parents or children who are opposed are actually starting to think you might back down on this one.

D. **Crunch time**

This is the moment when confidence in the change is at its lowest. You could well be the only person who still believes this is right. I love this time – it means it is about to start working, confidence is about to rise, you are going to achieve this. It is the moment when you need to be gutsy and have confidence in your high expectations of what you and your school can do. If you have planned properly, and already judged this change to be achievable, then it is and you will achieve it.

E. **Locked-in change**

This is when you arrive at the point when you can fairly confidently say that the school has achieved its strategic aim. Whatever that aim was, students will be in a better school as a result. No one will ever mention the crunch time, by the way.

Key points

- Plan before the launch (afterwards never really works too well)
- Be ready for crunch time
- Credit the team for their accomplishments
- Take the blame and give the credit (not the other way around)

Sorting out dealing with complaints

As a new head teacher, it didn't feel right to me that parents thought they had an automatic right to see me. I even became a bit high and mighty, comparing myself to a bank manager, for example, who presumably would not lower himself to come down to the floor of the bank. *I could not have been more wrong.* Following a brainwave from our chair of governors, we turned the desire of some parents to see the head teacher into a huge strength, which is what you have to do with any situation. For the past four years I have, in fact, guaranteed parents a direct line to the head teacher. I am proud to be able to offer this.

Parents want to be reassured, as we all do. Overnight we were able to turn a situation around by offering the ultimate reassurance: if parents write, email or phone I personally call them back within twenty-four hours and, if they still want a meeting, this is guaranteed to take place within three days, invariably sooner. This is an incredibly confident and supportive line to take. It has worked brilliantly for me.

One of parents' biggest complaints (i.e. you can never see the head) is now non-existent in our school. This approach also helps me to keep in touch when dealing with parents, and probably keeps other members of staff on their toes too. In some schools head teachers often only see the parents who pretty much force their way in, which is blatantly unfair to other parents and sends out a message that shouting loudly is rewarded.

The obvious danger with this tactic is that the head teacher will be swamped. In actual fact, requests to see me have plummeted, probably because disgruntled parents were angrier at a school which they perceived to be not listening (even though we were!). Like the rest of us, they wanted to be taken seriously, to be 'honoured'. On average, I probably have to phone one or two parents a week and have meetings with one or two a month as a result of this offer. Ironically, both of these totals are far less than the numbers I was seeing before all parents had equal, guaranteed access!

I do see the odd complainant for something that someone else in our school could have dealt with, but it is a small price to pay. Instead, I get to learn about one more student and perhaps to them the issue is not so trivial.

The most important part is getting back in touch when you promised to. When the parent answers the phone you can hear their anger dissipate. People want to be listened to and taken seriously. It seems pretty reasonable, doesn't it?

If a complaint comes through to you:

1. Phone to say when you will respond to them by
2. Talk to the member(s) of staff concerned
3. Get back to them by that date
4. Give them the school's view

Remember, the burden of proof is lower in schools than in courts – your role is to come to a judgement about what happened, not to prove anything.

Finally, by making yourself available, if something has gone wrong you'll get to know about it sooner and be able to apologise – before making sure it doesn't happen again!

Key points

- Guarantee the right for all parents to see you
- Listen but do not always agree
- Deal with complaints fairly and honestly
- Remember that no one wants their children to fail: we are all on the same side

---

Sorting out rewards

Positive behavioural change is definitely more likely to happen if a school has a good, vibrant rewards system which has genuine integrity in the eyes of the students. I have read that the ratio of positive to negative consequences should be three to one. If we combine our rewards system, letters home, celebration assemblies and everything else, our ratio is probably fifty to one positive, maybe higher.

It now seems incredible that we used to spend over £100,000 every year on the tiny minority of our students who were failing with us. Moving just a fraction of this amount into our rewards budget was a great, symbolic moment on our journey to improve behaviour around the school.

Key points

- Institute a rewards system
- Monitor its use to ensure it is fair and consistent
- Remember that rewards are more likely to improve behaviour than any negatives

---

Sorting out uniform

There are two schools of thought for new head teachers who want to deal with uniform: try to do everything at once or do it one stage at a time. Rightly or wrongly, I chose the latter and have been pleased with the progress made.

It is always worth getting to grips with what your students are wearing – it is a very powerful symbol of the school. Whether accurate and fair, or not, this is how large sections of the community will judge your school.

Be warned, though – this is the shallow end of the pool. Nothing wakes people up more than uniform and you'll be pleased to know there will be thousands of experts out there.

When I arrived, I was struck by the number of students wearing white trainers, mainly because 'their families couldn't afford shoes', which is usually nonsense. I was also astonished at the number of facial piercings on show. However, using a systematic approach – and working out that separating Year 11 students from their eyebrow bars would arguably be more difficult than it was worth – we committed to the phasing out of all piercings from the following September and pledged to get rid of white trainers from day one, which we did. (A top tip is to send letters or flyers to local businesses that do piercings, pointing out that these are not allowed in your school.)

This type of work is not easy and someone will oppose everything you do, but the more headway you make, the easier it becomes. Within a few weeks of having got a feel for the school, I was able to put a large number of uniform concerns on the behavioural timeline, most of which we mopped up by the beginning of the second year of adopting this approach. By the third year, we were so confident that we made the decision to move to a more traditional uniform of blazers, shirts and ties, which has proved to be successful.

When students or parents tell you that it doesn't matter what they wear, it is worth pointing out that even if there was no uniform, a school would still require a dress code. Innocently ask them, 'Is it the rule you don't agree with or the fact that we're applying it to your daughter?' When they tell me it's 'pathetic', I always agree, and ask why they are making an issue out of it in that case.

The only way to change attitudes decisively, of course, is to maintain a very simple response. We stopped accepting notes from home: mum might have not have written it and what she wants might not be what you think is fair anyway. The other problem with notes from home is that you are on the back foot. Tomorrow you won't even get a note, just a request to phone home. If you want to tie up your morning doing that, good luck. I don't.

There is no doubt that becoming less tolerant has transformed our mornings; in fact, they have changed beyond recognition. Mornings used to be quite stressful and a waste of everyone's time. Now, instead of being dominated by taxing, make-it-up-as-you-go-along decisions about uniform, we can enjoy assemblies, talk to students as they arrive and pop into tutor groups to see their work. Which is what we really should have been doing all along, before we were held to ransom by a tiny minority of parents who thought the rules only applied to everyone else.

So how did we do it? Basically, by being strategic, patient, going for the quick wins first and treating everyone the same.

Key points

- Pick the most obvious and achievable problems first
- Be strategic – decide this term's focus, next term's and so on
- Take students off timetable if they are not in the correct uniform
- Regularly review your timeline to ensure earlier improvements are still in place

Sorting out belief

Belief is better than hope. Everyone is looking to you for inspiration and guidance. You *can* do these things.

Sorting out fixed-term exclusions

Fixed-term exclusions can be an absolute disaster for schools. In fact, as the almost ultimate sanction they are a curious one, because the school is seeking to deprive the student of the one thing that could make a difference in their lives. Thoughts about the wisdom of fixed-term exclusions go to the heart of the philosophy of school behaviour management. I have found the subject to be a very emotive one, with many colleagues sounding like Charlton Heston on gun ownership: 'I have only five words for you: from my cold, dead hands.'

If our aim is to improve the behaviour of individual students, then we have to ask ourselves whether or not fixed-term exclusions actually work. If the same students from your school are regularly sent home, the answer might well be no. Fixed-term exclusions send the student back to where the problem often originated and away from where the answer ought to lie. They alienate parents. They create a highly visible platform for a student who has done something wrong – in fact, something seriously wrong. (Also, have you ever noticed how many excluded students there are at the school gate throughout the day as well as at the end of the day?) These guys are there to be seen – it is critical for their self-esteem. Often they are closer to their school than they might have been on a normal day! And then there is the work they ought to have been doing – how often is that done properly and returned? And what do you do if it isn't – exclude them again?

For me, the most serious reason why fixed-term exclusions don't work is that the student doesn't have to do anything – they don't have to consent to any part of the process. It is easy to be dismissive about something which is done *to you*. The power, and the change, comes when we have to be a part of the consequence to make it work. Which approach made me a safer driver: the fixed-penalty fine or the driver awareness course?

If a school is unwilling or not yet ready to move away from fixed-term exclusions, I would suggest they all at least implement some form of internal exclusion (see page 26). An interview with a senior member of staff before they return to school is also absolutely essential, so there is at least a part of the overall consequence that the student actually has to do themselves.

Key questions

- Does sending children home work for your school?
- How do you know?
- Is there a better alternative?
- If so, what is stopping you going for it?

Sorting out an inclusion room

The inclusion room is without doubt the jewel in the crown of my approach to improving whole-school behaviour. Even after more than three years, I pop in and wonder how we coped without a consequence which was so reasonable, fair and *absolutely* non-negotiable.

Why does an inclusion room work so well?

- It applies to all students
- It operates with absolute certainty
- It is reasonable
- It keeps students safe
- Parents much prefer it
- Students don't like it (kind of important as consequences go)
- Students have to consent to it – at no time is their attendance or work effort forced
- Students continue to learn

A word of warning: there will be children in your school who have effortlessly knocked down or circumnavigated every barrier or consequence that has been put in their way since they were born. They have won every time. They have worn down everyone around them, many of whom no longer even try to deal with their behaviour and who have instead waved the white flag and chosen a quiet life (some chance!). These students might not like the inclusion room. Senior teachers must stand firm, each and every time.

So how does it work?

The inclusion room is a supervised room within the school (not a hut on the far perimeter) where students work in silence for the same number of days as they would have received a fixed-term exclusion. They can have one or two formal warnings during the day, after which they have failed to complete the day in the inclusion room to the required standard and therefore have to re-do the day.

The person in charge of the inclusion room is crucial: they cannot be sergeant majorish but nor can they go for the 'let's rap or write poetry about your problems' approach. To be clear, I'm not knocking either strategy – we do both at different times – but the inclusion room is *not* the place for it. The person who runs the room must be able to walk a very narrow path at all times: simply upholding the values of the inclusion room to all students, without fear or favour. No deals, no winks, no cut corners, no raised voices: work properly and quietly (not an outrageous demand in a school) or fail and we'll see you tomorrow.

Our room is light and quiet, it is situated in the heart of the school and it has desks and chairs separated by screens. It operates on the same timetable as the school day, although breaks and lunch are taken at different times. Students are escorted to the toilet and, of course, they are not allowed to go anywhere on their own during the day. They will try, however, because it is essential for them to be seen by their peers.

Many students actually don't mind the inclusion room once they accept that it is going to happen: it can act as a pit-stop, allowing them to leave their carefully crafted persona at the door, escape the peer pressure and actually refocus on learning – which is why we're all here in the first place.

If a student repeatedly fails the inclusion room, there are two choices: the inclusion room goes or the student goes. Leadership is very tough sometimes.

OK, so why doesn't every school do this?

- They might not know about it
- They might not be able to afford it (fixed-term exclusions are cheap: they only cost a stamp)
- They might not be confident they could hold the line

Key points

- Pick the right person to be in charge of your inclusion room
- Run fixed-term inclusions as formally and as seriously as fixed-term exclusions, including the paperwork
- Do not allow students to be 'dropped in' – entry and exit must be planned
- Work through the initial resistance

Sorting out what a school can look like that hasn't got it right

In schools where behaviour is not yet successfully, and strategically, managed, you might see some of these:

- All the colours of the rainbow can be found in the various complicated report cards that are handed out
- Consequences might happen to some students, sometimes
- Students on report get privileges (e.g. they can miss lessons to walk around the school looking for their report card)
- Events recorded on the cards are not followed up
- The students know a lot more about what is happening than the teachers
- The parents know a lot more about what is happening than the teachers
- On-call assistance is non-existent or unreliable
- Students who have chosen to behave badly are returned to the same class
- There are periodic blitzes (e.g. on ties, make-up, lateness) which last for five minutes, sometimes even longer
- Senior teachers are rarely seen
- Staff are left to make it up as they go along
- There is a profound acceptance of poor behaviour

- The minority of negative students receive the vast majority of the attention (which compounds their negativity)
- Teachers are only confident to teach within safety limits

Sorting out sin bins

By sin bins, I mean rooms where students can be 'dropped in' for various lengths of time and for various reasons. I dislike them. Here's why:

- They tie up important staff and space
- The person running it could do a lot more for your school working as a full-time head of year
- Students will secretly arrange to meet there
- Students will possibly quite like being there (this is probably not a good thing for what is supposed to be a sanction)
- Although getting students into the room should be easy enough, getting them back into lessons – on your terms – could prove a tad tricky

Sorting out the Ten Commandments

1. Thou shalt not send students home nor reward them with biscuits and cosy chats in your office

2. Thou shalt not let students walk around the school unsupervised

3. Thou shalt have the same rules for everyone and not do deals with individual students or parents

4. Thou shalt not undermine teachers by failing to support them

5. Thou shalt not believe that families can afford brand new trainers but not shoes

6. Thou shalt devise a straightforward, manageable behaviour management system that staff can consistently use

7. Thou shalt leave thy office regularly

8. Thou shalt be consistent and fair

9. Thou shalt model thy expectations

10. Thou shalt always try to improve behaviour in thy school

Sorting out dealing with 'difficult' parents

There are three ways to deal with parents. The first two are:

1. Hide

2. Do deals

The trouble with these options is that they aren't very effective. However, the good news is that there is a third way ...

Although the whole '85% of communication is non-verbal' idea is accepted as being, well, rubbish, there are nevertheless some important approaches you can use to lower the tension in a situation. One of these is not to sit between the parent and the door – you don't want them feeling blocked in (and if it goes wrong, a smooth exit is better for all parties, believe me!).

Once everyone is seated, offer drinks – for some reason it is much harder to be annoyed when you're holding a cup and saucer. Perhaps it is a deep-rooted sense of the absurd. Who knows? Who cares? It seems to work. Biscuits can also be a powerful strategic ally in these situations, but obviously not those you could use to point with provocatively, chocolate fingers, for example.

First of all, *agree the facts*. This is the tough bit and will require a very strong hand on the reins at times. Everyone must agree what actually happened. It is probable you weren't there and it is unlikely the parent was either. Do not let the narrative wander away. The meeting is only about one item or one item at a time. It is not about rumours, past incidents, problems outside school and so on. Take time to establish and to agree what actually happened. Achieving this can be hard but the meeting is almost doomed to be a pointless, negative, free-for-all, spinning out of control, if this crucial stage is not done first and to completion.

'I' statements are great at any time (for example, 'I felt threatened,' or 'I was embarrassed') but especially when confirming how a child behaved. Do not get confrontational yourself. Assertive, yes. Confrontational, no.

I also strongly feel that parents should never be allowed to interrogate the teacher. I am always dismayed to hear of instances when a poor teacher is put in the dock to be cross-examined by a parent. To spell it out: *I* do the investigating. *I* do any apologising.

A great line to use with parents is: 'Before we start, can I just say that I'm not sitting here saying that our school is perfect or that we always get everything right.' Another one is: 'It's important to remember that neither of us were there.'

Make notes while they are talking – it looks like you're actually listening. But *actually* listen. If you need to glance at your watch, do it while you are talking, not them – it's a lot less rude.

I know that to many, letting disgruntled parents 'sound off' about anything or anyone they don't like is a good solution.

My concern is about what we are actually consenting to – I don't want to be in a position where wholesale criticism of the school and its staff is taking place. 'Letting them get everything off their chests' also risks losing control of the meeting, especially the agenda you should be mentally working through and sticking to.

Even on the phone, I have asked our receptionist to do the following if a parent is abusive:

1. Say 'Mr Rowe has told us not to accept phone calls like this. You will need to get in touch with him.'
2. Put the phone down.

Any guesses as to whether we get more or less abusive phone calls now? It's all about choice.

It can be very effective to steer the conversation away from their particular child by reminding a parent that the meeting is actually about the school's values rather than one individual student. A frank line to take if you are accused of not listening is to say that you are listening, but you do not agree.

It is important to remember the importance of the role of a senior teacher in a secondary school. We sometimes forget the huge power and influence we have. Parents don't and it can be very intimidating – an emotion we all express in different ways. Meeting somewhere less formal that the 'Head Teacher's Office' can sometimes raise the chances of a successful meeting, as parents are less likely to feel like naughty children themselves.

As a professional, it is important to know what you want out of the meeting. My basic approaches are either to apologise if we have genuinely made a mistake, to get back to them at a later date if I can't resolve the problem then and there, or to decide that the school has behaved properly and tell them that. Occasionally a parent will say 'you can't prove that' of the famous 'at the end of the day, it's the teacher's word against his' conundrum. This is actually correct. It is important to remember, however, that you are not operating within a court room. A school does not have to prove what happened. Your job is to review the facts and come up with a judgement, nothing more.

Whatever the type of meeting, and however you decide to play it, the result to aim for must be an encounter ending in agreement and a handshake.

Finally, please remember that some of these meetings will go wrong anyway. The strategies outlined above will increase the chances of a good, professional conversation taking place, but with so many external factors swirling around, nothing can guarantee success.

Key points

- Meet the parents
- Agree the facts
- Don't allow them to cross-examine a member of staff
- *You* do any apologising
- You do not have to prove anything
- Remember, you're the professional

Sorting out home visits

There are three responses to the problem of parents who don't answer the phone if the school number appears on the display:

- Give up (this isn't recommended)
- Use a different phone – parents will often suddenly be in
- Visit in person

Home visits can be hugely powerful – in over ten years of doing them, I have never had to visit the same household more than once. I initially thought the school would be on the back foot in a parent's home but the exact opposite is true. By bothering to turn up you have confounded their expectations and visibly – and powerfully – reinforced the view that actually the values of your school are important; so important in fact, that you will do what you feel is necessary to uphold them. Reluctant parents hate the idea of members of school staff appearing at their front door, and it is worth the effort just to see the horrified look on Amy's face as she comes downstairs to see the two of you sitting on the sofa.

Ultimately, it comes down to how much you believe in what you are doing. My experience is that being prepared to go the extra mile in this way reaps enormous dividends.

Important note: Never do a home visit without letting your school know where you are going, never go on your own and never take a risk with your own safety. If it doesn't feel right, leave it – you can't win them all.

Key points

- Make some home visits
- Tell the office where you are going and take a phone
- Never go alone or take any risks

Sorting out the reasons not to try to improve behaviour

There are two main excuses for not addressing challenging behaviour:

1. It can't be done

2. It is hassle

The first is false and the second is true, although it can be quite fun too, as well as being absolutely right for *all* your children.

Sorting out the reasons to try to improve behaviour

There are many incentives to tackle challenging behaviour, including:

- It is rewarding
- It is right
- Life will become easier
- Results will improve
- All children will be happier

Sorting out guarantees to students

Our school is very proud of the assurances we make to our students. You get a guarantee of what you can expect when you buy a kettle, so is it unreasonable for our students to have a set of expectations they can rely on too?

Ours are:

- I will personally reply within twenty-four hours of a parent getting in touch
- Following this, a meeting with me will be arranged within three days, if required
- Regular homework will be set in all subjects
- A wide choice of subjects will be available to all students
- A wide range of extra-curricular activities will be offered to students

Sorting out guarantees to staff

Let's be honest, you can't do anything without a good working relationship with colleagues. At our school we guarantee:

- Behavioural support will be offered at all times
- All emails to the head teacher will be replied to
- Staff have direct access to the head teacher
- Cover will be kept at virtually zero
- Staff well-being is an important school value and priority

We also don't mind if teachers leave school during planning, preparation and assessment (PPA) time, we never ask them to cover for colleagues unless there are genuine, unforeseen circumstances and, where possible, we encourage all members of staff to attend their own children's/grandchildren's school events during the day.

Sorting out what you can do with students on the edge of the precipice

A US comedian asks what unarmed British police shout at assailants who ignore them and keep running: 'Stop, or I'll shout stop again.' Does it feel like that sometimes with your trickiest students?

We all know them: the students who have turned over more new leaves than the Cuban cigar industry. The ones for whom everything has failed but they're still walking among us, picking and choosing which lessons they will decide to behave in and sticking two fingers up to your school's values. They can be quite reasonable sometimes, it's just that some rules aren't really for them and they'd rather not conform, if it's okay with you. The apparent immunity of these students is a very common complaint across schools.

These students are important because they've sussed out that there's actually nothing the school can do. Or they think there isn't ... I hope this book is giving you a few ideas to ensure that *all* your students work within the school's behavioural expectations. I would particularly recommend the inclusion room, home visits and a week of study focus for the most hard-to-reach individuals, but it's your choice.

What a school absolutely cannot have are students who are blatantly and highly visibly choosing not to consent to the school's values. They are a walking, talking guarantee that your ambitions to improve behaviour will fail, which ... um ... is what they want.

The difficult part of this equation is that you might end up having to move students on. We do this very reluctantly and only when all else has failed, but for me a choice between one student and the values of our school is one I have to be prepared to take.

Key points

- Aim high
- Treat everyone the same

Sorting out the behaviour management policy

Without a shadow of doubt, the behaviour management policy is the most important document in your school. It is critical and must be completely up to date, which means establishing a way of ensuring that the relevant governing body committee gives the policy regular approval.

The job of the governing body is to ensure the school's policies – which the governors are responsible for creating – are applied consistently. Which they should be. If they're right in the first place, they're all you need.

Incidentally, my personal view is that recent legislation has helped the pendulum to swing back in favour of schools being able to uphold good behavioural standards, which is a good move.

Key points

- Ensure your school's behaviour management policy accurately reflects what you are doing
- Keep it regularly updated
- Stick to it

Sorting out study focus

Undoubtedly, study focus is one of the very important parts of behaviour management. This is a big play, so don't start unless you are prepared to finish!

Initially, ask teachers to nominate the students who are persistently difficult in their lessons. Just being asked will be a relief to some staff. When they realise that something is actually going to happen they will be delighted.

The half-dozen or so students with the most nominations then spend a week working separately from the rest of the school, in silence, with separate breaks and lunchtimes. The room should be supervised by your best staff when it comes to behaviour. Like the inclusion room, this is the students' opportunity to prove they deserve their place in the school. If possible, it is a great idea to get parents on board too. Be warned: some of the students selected might not be too happy about this.

Here's the really powerful bit: while students are in study focus, all of their classmates fill in a short questionnaire summarising how different their lessons are without their disruptive peers. On the final day, each study focus student has a meeting at which these questionnaires – there should be hundreds by the end of the week – are shown to them. Be prepared for the students to be shocked; this will almost certainly be the first time they will have been confronted by the fact that other students in the school don't like how they are behaving. Often they despise it. So they should – and a school's acceptance of poor behaviour is damaging their lives. Remember, even if students on the receiving end get upset, this could be as nothing compared to how distraught other pupils might be on results day because the behaviour of this minority has caused them to fail. It all comes down to who you are working for.

Key points

- Only use study focus when you feel you can do it properly and confidently
- Ensure plenty of questionnaires are filled in
- Keep parents informed
- Be certain of what you will do if a student chooses to fail

---

Sorting out alternative education

The Department for Education's behavioural expert, Charlie Taylor, recently produced a report which contained several criticisms of the relationship between schools and some alternative education placements.[*] It was difficult not to agree with his findings. The ballooning use of 'other providers' – and the associated billions of pounds of public funds they cost – is an area which would undoubtedly benefit from light being shed on it. This would both uncover what works well and expose what I have no doubt are some 'less rigorous' outfits who are taking the money and running. I have visited providers where four students, supported by four members of staff, were doing very little and with the inevitable blind eye being turned to smoking, truancy and failure. Actually, I say they weren't doing much – I think one of them was making toast ...

Here's a tricky question. Do you think, for Christmas, the course:

1. Finished on the same day as local schools?

2. Carried on even longer?

3. Finished a week before?

The problem for society is that these children do not go away. They grow up (although a sad minority don't even manage

---

[*]Charlie Taylor, *Taylor Review of alternative provision*. London: Department for Education, 2012. Available at www.education.gov.uk/schools/pupilsupport/behaviour/b00204776/taylor-review-of-alternative-provision (accessed 18 March 2013).

that) to lead difficult lives and often have children who are highly likely to fail themselves. Much has been written about these students. The economic and social costs of their educational failure are incalculable – and are paid for by all of us. This must end; society literally cannot afford it. It is time for action.

When I arrived at the school we were spending over £100,000 a year on alternative placements for students we couldn't cope with internally. Although I bitterly hated spending this money, it was clear that the best way to end it was to improve behaviour to a point where we didn't need it. This is why we continued to pay out (through gritted teeth) for alternative provision for the first two years.

In the past, 'hard to reach' pupils (the course might actually have been called that!) used to pop off and do some canoeing during the school day. Like all schools, we have a great many students who deal with serious difficulties in their lives, but most of them do not take it out on the school. I wonder what these pupils thought when they watched this small group load up and drive off for a day out? Contempt? Disgust? I've met one or two of the canoeists since – they're not doing much these days. They can't believe the money that was thrown at them either.

I passionately believe that good behaviour and the right choices should be rewarded. Not only does it seem fairer, it works too.

Over 99% of last year's Year 11 students are now in education, employment or training – a record for our school.

Key points

- ■ Be careful that you are not inadvertently rewarding negative behaviour
- ■ Rewards which are not earned aren't worth much
- ■ Audit the quality of other providers you work with
- ■ Aim to reduce the amount of alternative provision

Sorting out the on-call rota

A well-organised on-call system is undoubtedly one of the cheapest, easiest and most effective win-wins a school can introduce. Here's how to give your on-call system a tune up.

Record when the on-call system is used. This provides great data for working out if problems centre on individual students, boys or girls, certain physical locations, particular teachers having difficulties and so on. Knowing what the problem is certainly gives you more chance to improve it.

Use as many different members of staff as possible. This delivers great training, empowers individuals and gives them a whole-school view. It also, critically, sends out a message that all members of staff can do discipline. Just using senior teachers ties them up and also says 'we do discipline, not these other teachers'. This is a mistake. As well as monopolising key members of staff, this approach automatically relegates everyone else's skills in the eyes of the students. The final irony, of course, is that the school's senior management team are probably not all endowed with superhuman powers. Some will be good and some not so, like any team of teachers.

Train up new team members. This doesn't need to be hugely extensive – just take them through the basics. It is certainly worth shadowing new members of the on-call rota for their first incidents.

One essential that all on-call staff must learn is not to undermine the class teacher by throwing open the swing doors of the saloon like a Wild West sheriff, showing off how strict they are by taking down a couple of outlaws and then blowing the smoke from the end of their gun and leaving, feeling pretty darn good about life. This is actually a disaster, as the teacher left behind has been branded 'helpless'. Good luck with the rest of the lesson ...

Other on-call tips include:

- Don't allow the teacher to take ages explaining what has happened. The best words of advice at this point are: 'Carry on teaching'. If not, the room can turn into an emotionally charged kangaroo court
- If the teacher wants a student to be removed, even if you feel the situation could be resolved, take them away. It isn't fair to undermine the teacher and this action could also chip away at the seriousness with which the on-call system might be regarded, by teachers and students
- As the teacher carries on teaching, sit next to the student the teacher wants to be removed. Do not speak for three minutes, then silently motion them outside. Don't bring them back
- Don't get emotional – it is a 'guardian of the values' type role
- Don't necessarily judge the student too harshly – they are children not criminals

- Don't judge the teacher too harshly – they might have got it wrong, they might not have. Teachers rely on the integrity of their school's approach to behaviour, and your school relies on them to enact it

You can't win them all. Stuff happens. If you hit a brick wall when doing on-call and you can't resolve a situation, then get someone else in!

Key points

- Record the use of the on-call system
- Allow a wide range of staff to take part
- Always remove a student if the teacher asks

Sorting out that prevention is better than cure

The basic philosophy of a school should always be to stop something bad from happening, rather than dealing with the consequences. A robust, consistent and fair approach to behaviour, enacted by all staff, set out clearly in the behavioural policy, with a good on-call system, all staff doing their duties properly, rigorous detentions and a leadership group walking the walk will lead to students having confidence in their school. And, ultimately, there will be many fewer problems.

Sorting out whole-school detentions

The way school detentions are run sometimes makes you wonder why schools bother. Perhaps they don't realise the huge danger of running a system that has more holes in it than an Atlantic fishing net. If your approach to detentions – whether whole-school, left up to individuals or departmental – is seriously flawed, the students will be running rings around you. That's not good. In fact, it is a morale-sapping, counter-productive disaster.

On the question of detentions, I am convinced that, at least in our school, running whole-school detentions, and no other type, is the only is the way to go. Relying on different departments or individual teachers to operate with the required consistency is hugely risky, because as an approach it is highly unlikely to deliver. Without leadership, not a lot can. At the very least, there would be huge inconsistency in how sanctions are applied.

Anything other than a centralised, whole-school detentions system has a high chance of being an absolute catastrophe. However, the strategy must include all teachers, otherwise a 'hierarchical' message is being sent out (i.e. senior teachers are more important and powerful) which can make life tricky for everyone else.

If your school is going to run detentions, they *must* be run properly. Here are some of the holes you'll sometimes find in the net:

- Children who are away on the day of the detention are not followed up
- The detention is never actually set, even though the teacher thinks it has been
- Nothing happens if the detention isn't served
- The detention occurs so many weeks after the initial problem that the student genuinely doesn't have a clue why they are there
- Heads of year and/or senior teachers cancel detentions: they tell the student but not the teacher who set it

If a child due in detention can walk past the teacher on duty with a cheery wave, then the whole school must be laughing behind your backs. So the choice is either to run detentions appropriately or to abandon them. Anything in between is a dangerous tightrope.

Besides, detentions themselves aren't so bad. They are an opportunity for a student to hold their hands up and say 'I did it, and this is me putting it right'.

So what does our system look like?

- Teachers (or any member of staff) give two formal warnings first (C1, C2) before issuing a detention (C3). These are recorded so they can be monitored

- A letter is automatically sent home, generated by admin staff not teachers, meaning the detention will be served as soon as possible. The letter includes the sentence 'or on the first school day following absence' which deals with one of the ways out of it
- Students receive a reminder just before the end of the school day
- Staff on duty at the exits and supervising the buses have a list of who is in detention, including what bus each student gets on (absent students are removed from the list and added to the next day's)
- A cross-section of staff supervise the detention – it is essential that students see that we are all equally important
- If a student doesn't turn up, their name is automatically put on the next day's list. They will be doubly inconvenienced by doing a lunchtime detention the next day too. Where possible, we also phone home just after the start of the detention to try to get the student returned to us, which makes a point to parents
- Ultimately, if a student does choose to miss a detention, like all of our approaches, we never have to panic – they will be picked up the next day

For us, whole-school detentions have proved to be a highly effective way of sending out a very powerful message. Be warned, though – it's not for the fainthearted. Oh, and some students might be really unhappy about it.

Key points

- Whole school detentions are the best and fairest system
- These should not be 'senior team' detentions, unless you want the students to think that you have a higher status and are more important
- Absent students and those who 'forget' *must* do the detention

Sorting out the relationship with the governing body

The relationship between a school's senior team and its governing body, and in particular between the head teacher and the chair of governors, is a critical one. A bit of warmth and mutual respect is good for the school.

However, in terms of support for the school's behavioural work, the role of the governing body is actually very straightforward: it is to ensure that the values of the school, as set out in its policies, are adhered to.

I believe in people's right to complain and to seek redress. Similarly, I believe in robust, decent values being applied equally to everyone, without fear or favour.

Captain Jean-Luc Picard put it best: 'You'll get no special treatment on my ship.'

Sorting out what you can do to improve your school as a senior teacher

Anything, really.

Sorting out toilets

Toilets are the most reliable metaphor, and the greatest test, for the effectiveness and genuine care shown in a school.

Although much had been improved in the school where I became head teacher, the toilets were not one of them. We started with the girls' toilets. Beforehand they were intimidating, badly decorated areas, with overflowing sanitary bins and no locks on the doors. Within a couple of weeks they were pink, had mirrors with lights around them, hand-cream, flowers and pictures. That was four years ago. There has never been a problem since.

So how did we do it? What worked for us was allocating a few thousand pounds (the resulting drop in vandalism more than covered it) to a group of students, and then putting their ideas into practice.

It is essential that toilets are:

- Regularly checked
- As open as possible
- Clean
- Well-stocked
- Safe

There are still stories of students who don't go to the toilet all day in some schools. Heartbreaking – someone ought to do something about it ...

Sorting out hierarchy

Many disruptive students bounce around for years making teachers' lives a misery, but are only excluded when they have the audacity to swear at the head teacher. I believe that everyone in school should be afforded the same rights, dignity and protection.

Are we really saying to students that it is OK to swear at Sue in the kitchen but not a member of the senior team? Who decided that? What an incredible message to give out! Poor old Sue!

While we're on the subject, it can be incredible what some staff will accept, behaviourally. This is dangerous and needs to be challenged. Fast. Similarly, make sure that anyone who comes in to work with the students also has a pep talk about what is and isn't acceptable. I've met people who are so 'down with the kids' it's unbelievable. Great for them (arguably), but a potential disaster for the school's values and an inconsistent message for the students too.

Sorting out the fire drill

Working hard to plan and deliver a silent fire drill was undoubtedly the best possible start we could have had in our campaign to improve student behaviour across the school.

The fire drill is normally the only time the whole school is together in one place. Something to dread? No, a golden opportunity. Fire drills are going to happen anyway so, like all aspects of school life, you should use them to get across your message and values. A slick, efficient fire drill, with students lining up in silence, is an incredible opportunity; if you don't use it to show who is in charge, you can rest assured that a minority of students will. The moral high ground for doing it properly could not be clearer either – children will be safer as they exit the school more quickly and calmly.

When I joined my school and announced we would do the fire drill in silence I could see, and have heard anecdotally since, that the majority view was that I had gone mad! However, I knew we could do it and I knew that doing it would speak volumes about our intentions, as well as put a rocket under our expectations of the school.

So how did we do it? If we had not felt confident we could achieve a whole-school silent fire drill, we would have held one separately for older students (if they were the problem) somewhere else. We then would have sorted out the younger ones, and aimed to bring them both together after a term, or a year, recorded that in our behavioural timeline and stuck to it.

My philosophy was simple: there was no pressure on me at all. My job on the day was going to be watching our two excellent deputy head teachers to ensure they pulled it off. If they had any sense – which they do – they would put their expectations on the senior teachers they link with, who, in turn, should be watching their heads of year to make sure they were doing everything needed to ensure success. A good head of year would be making certain that form tutors were doing it right and, of course, a great form tutor would have drilled their students beforehand – even marching them onto the field to rehearse – and would have stressed that lining up properly, in silence, is the responsibility of each individual student.

At all levels of the school, members of staff put in time to ensure that staff and students took responsibility for playing their part. Even so, I could see that some individuals were genuinely unsure that we could get the whole school out, in time, and have them standing in straight, silent lines. At this point I remember telling them, in a staff briefing, that I had no doubt that we could do this, because I had no doubt in the quality of the people in the room who would make it happen. If that meant that I had more confidence in them than anyone else, I didn't mind that. In fact, I felt it was a good place for a head teacher to be.

I would debate whether or not we should aim to make the fire drill silent, orderly and safe. What I would not debate was whether or not we could do it. Obviously I could not have been sure that we would pull it off first time. If that was the case, we would have reviewed it, altered what was necessary and done it again. After all, it is us who decide what type of school we are going to be, not a minority of students or staff who don't agree with the changes.

And then we came to the day. I walked out into the centre of the playing field and waited for the bell to ring. Moments later, the whole school began to emerge onto the school field. Silently, they lined up in neat rows, expertly marshalled by hard-working form tutors. I had witnessed the fastest and safest fire drill I had ever seen. Don't get me wrong. I acted all calm and matter of fact, but inside I felt genuine pride at what this fantastic team had just achieved. I was also excited – the dam had burst. If we could achieve this by working together systematically and with the highest possible expectations of ourselves and of our students, we could do incredible things. And we did.

Members of staff even came up to me afterwards to thank me, which, thinking about it now, is remarkable. Perhaps they needed to see what could be achieved by working together. Either way, we never looked back.

Achieving a silent fire drill was undoubtedly the beginning of our work to take behaviour to the next level. The fire alarm has not been set off in the four years since. However, now I've just written that, it probably will tomorrow!

Key points

- Plan the drill carefully
- Make sure everyone knows what their responsibility is
- Have students facing away, not towards each other
- Put older students somewhere else if you need to achieve this in stages
- Keep going – it's worth it

Sorting out letting students leave the building during the school day

Basically, don't let students leave during school hours. Each student out and about is a walking billboard, telling local people that the school condones smoking, eating junk food, not being safe around cars and being vulnerable to untrustworthy adults.

In terms of reputation, the actions of some of them will literally be killing your school. It is easier to let them out but it is not the right thing to do.

If the culture has always been to allow students to wander off at lunchtimes, it might be wise to phase it out in stages. For example:

1. Decide a start date and record it on your behavioural timeline

2. Only let Year 11 students out from that date. Monitor, patrol outside the school and insist on passes being shown (which can be confiscated)

3. Once this cohort leave the school, end the practice completely

Sorting out a behaviour timeline

Improving the behaviour in your school is important. I can't imagine setting out on any course of action without a plan. No plan = reactive. Plan = proactive.

Our timeline is as simple as we can make it and serves two purposes. The first is to look forwards, to ensure that we are constantly looking for ways to further improve, even if these have by now come down to marginal gains in some areas. Secondly, it is critical in allowing us to look backwards, to make certain that the changes we have brought in and the improvements we have made remain in place.

It also means that you can say to other people, and to yourself, no, we are not tackling that this term, but will be doing so from April. Knowing what is coming up also makes it easier to prepare and warn staff; plus, of course, the more you stick to and deliver the plan, the easier it becomes to improve your school.

There are certain times during the school year when launching an improvement is easier than others. The beginning of any term is great, the best being the start of the autumn term. My favourite – and it is sad to see schools that miss this chance to up their game – is the day after Year 11 leave. The school is ready and waiting for something new and you have a few weeks of the summer term to lock it in. From September, as new students join who have never known anything different, it will be as if the school has always done it this way.

I would therefore recommend that your annual behavioural timeline/plan has four main times: September, January, April and the Year 11 leaving date.

Some examples of changes we have brought in which feature on our behavioural timeline include:

- Black shoes only
- Consequences for being late
- Whole-school detentions
- No facial piercings
- All students bring the correct equipment to school

I once heard a great quote from a certain Dolly Parton: 'We cannot direct the wind but we can adjust the sails'. Nice one, Dolly.

The timeline is reviewed every half-term at our weekly senior management meetings, which in turn helps to keep the focus of these meetings strategic. Operational stuff is dealt with in the fifteen-minute daily senior team meetings which kick off each school day.

A behavioural timeline means you are improving your school strategically. It means that the decisions and direction are decided by you and not by the prevailing winds, background noise or those with the loudest voices. Some changes will be popular, some won't. That doesn't necessarily mean that they are more, or less, right.

An added bonus is that, once the school is used to the concept of a timeline, they will find the approach works equally well for other areas of school life, such as the school's partnership work with local primary schools, teaching and learning, and so on.

Key points

- ▨ Plan your timeline
- ▨ Stick to the plan
- ▨ Use the timeline to ensure previous higher standards are being maintained, as well as looking to the future
- ▨ Sometimes be patient, sometimes be impatient!

Sorting out students who arrive late in the mornings

I once worked in a school where the head teacher suddenly became irritated one morning about students arriving late. We all duly rushed out, administering stern looks and generally expressing disapproval. One or two of us even wrote down names but, of course, we didn't have a clue what to do with them. The next day we were there again and the number of late students had fallen slightly. On the third day we were back in the office. Those two days were never mentioned again and I would watch the students arriving late over the head teacher's shoulder as he was talking each morning.

Keen-eyed readers will have probably guessed that I didn't really approve of this approach. It actually seemed worse than doing nothing. When I had the chance, I assembled a group of staff – not all of whom were teachers – and set about trying to come up with a simple, workable and effective solution to the problem of latecomers. Incredibly, this took three meetings, which lasted five hours in total. Nailing down the specific problem – at what point does a student technically become late, where should they be and when – took forty-five minutes alone.

We know that groups of key individuals are likely to come up with better solutions than one person, especially when they are the members of staff who are directly involved. The approach we came up was incredibly successful and led us to begin to question more deeply whether or not we should be tolerating other negative aspects in the school.

So how did we do it? Two important decisions underpinned our approach:

1. All lateness had to be treated the same, regardless of how late a student was or the reason
2. The consequence had to be irritating rather than serious; clearly some students will be late for genuine reasons

We therefore devised a Kafkaesque form to be completed by all late students at breaktime. You know the sort of thing: name, date of birth, address including postcode, capital of Estonia, shoe size and so on. Anyone who failed to show up to fill in their form – despite their name being taken and being told by a member of the senior team at each school entrance – got a detention. What was crucial, however, was that the detention was for missing the breaktime form-filling session, not for actually being late. Heaven forbid ...

I was reminded of the power of language when a parent, dropping off their child late, asked me if he was in detention. 'No,' I said, 'don't worry – he's only got to fill in a form at breaktime.' 'That's alright then – no problem. Thanks.' The power of a word! Not using the word 'detention' completely changed the parent's stance.

Most lateness is occasional, but obviously the information this approach throws up will occasionally point to a serious safeguarding issue. Before we did this, parents might have thought their children were in school. We thought they were at home. Only the students knew where they were. It is impossible to calculate how much safer our students are as a result of this approach.

Finally, it is worth pointing out that lateness almost disappeared overnight, although maintaining this system is necessary to keep a lid on the odd one or two. Once you launch a new way of working you have to accept that it will almost definitely become part of school life. My advice is to accept it and start to see the profound benefits.

The strategy we used to crack lateness in the mornings also taught us that:

- Difficult problems require time to resolve properly: it is better for you to work out the flaws in the school's approach rather than an angry dad a week after you launch
- Often members of a working party will have slightly different views of the problem they are trying to resolve – this needs to be hammered out at the beginning
- We have a tendency to overload systems – there were a dozen extras which people wanted us to check each morning which would have caused the whole system to fall apart, including lateness itself

Key points

- Take the time to build a system that will hold water
- Define what 'late' actually means in your school
- Don't get into judging whether lateness is justified – treat everyone the same
- Develop an irritating consequence rather than a sanction
- Remember that a minority love the 'kudos' of being late
- Remember that being more vigilant can uncover safeguarding issues

Sorting out the 85% you can control now

There will always be events in school that are outside of your control, although I hope this book is helping you to come up with effective ways in which they can be improved too. Alongside these, however, is the bulk of work which is entirely down to us. Once you start adding it up, it is quite a list. There is easily enough here to allow you to define your school or redefine it if necessary. They are, in no particular order:

- Student council: there is literally no limit to how central and important this can be in your school
- Assemblies: well-organised, and often student-led, these can be used to reinforce the school's values – from entering in silence, to learning to praise each other and to accept praise
- Regular school newsletter
- The appearance of the school: flowers and hanging baskets, vibrant colours, displays, clean and safe toilets, etc.
- Working with the local press to ensure regular good news stories about your school appear: this is important for your school and helps to counteract the endless media slurs and prejudice about young people in general
- Books regularly marked
- Lessons starting on time

- Teacher absence addressed
- Uniform
- Fire drill
- Etc.

Note: I'd recommend brainstorming the work you do as a school – you'll be amazed at how much you already define!

Sorting out platforms

Platforms are anything positive which enables young people to have their say and to positively define their school. There is an army of fabulous young people just waiting for the chance to define your school. All they need is the signal from you and for the 'platforms' to define the school from to be built. Without these platforms, the tiny minority of difficult students will define your school. This is probably not a good thing for the rest of the school or for them.

The constant sound that must ring out is of the positives in your school. At our school we start our weekly senior team meetings with a 'good news' standing item. Unfortunately, however, the default for all of us is to focus on the negative. I have observed many lessons where ten minutes is lost directing the whole class to bask in the glow of Connor, who didn't bother to do his homework, while a dozen other Connors sit unrecognised, the gleaming homework in front of them barely noticed. Or Abbie, who gets more attention for not taking her coat off when asked than Jake, who has produced an immaculate piece of work. (A great tip here is for the teacher to thank everyone who has taken their coat off, possibly combined with a sideways glance at Abbie.) How much of your interaction with students is negative? Are they the students whose names you know?

So what platforms can we construct to enable the 99% of positive students to clamber aboard and help to define the school? Here are just a few:

- Whole-school awards evenings
- Awards evenings for students from local primary schools, held at the local church or cathedral (if you do posh)
- Weekly newsletter
- Prefects
- Celebration assemblies
- Student council
- Regular letters and phone calls home
- A rewards system
- A Hall of Fame: pictures of students doing brilliant things
- Teachers writing on the board the names of students who have done well, not badly
- Sending students to see the head teacher because their work is excellent

These platforms – and the many others out there – will electrify your school and make behavioural improvements so much easier.

Sorting out my ten favourite approaches

None of these approaches will work for long without a systematic process and they will all only improve issues, not eradicate them. The order in which you implement them will depend on how well you know your own school. In our school, weighing up impact against the time each improvement took, I would say the order of effectiveness for us was probably:

1. Inclusion room

2. Study focus

3. Lateness in the mornings

4. Whole-school detentions

5. Tracking behaviour

6. Changing the on-call system

7. Silent fire drill

8. Improvements to the decor and facilities around the school

9. Ensuring we had a behavioural timeline

10. Giving parents guaranteed access to the head teacher

Two of our biggest successes – phasing out fixed-term exclusions and paying for alternative education for students we couldn't contain – were consequences of these combined approaches, rather than being strategic aims in themselves.

We might have been able to achieve these both on day one, but without the rigorous values and robust consequences I would not have recommended it!

Sorting out full-time heads of year

I could not begin to imagine going back to a time when deputy head teachers, well-paid by the school to lead, took statements from students and dealt with endless, low-level issues. Dealt with, mind you, not resolved, because they were too busy dealing with these concerns in isolation to ever raise their heads above the parapet, get together and actually sort them out. Basically we were fire-fighting: endlessly reacting to events and constantly on the back foot. Riding out to meet problems, to challenge, change and improve our school has been so much more effective and enjoyable.

Moving to a system of full-time, non-teaching heads of year was one of the most important changes we made. As well as offering far better value, these are individuals who can resolve issues immediately, which leads to more prevention and less cure. They also work collaboratively, covering for each other when needed and cementing a common approach to problems.

Advertise for these positions and brilliant people will apply. They will come into your school and give 100%. Leaders will then be freed up to focus on improving the school.

If you don't feel you can afford to employ full-time heads of year, walk around and watch every person employed in your school who doesn't teach. Is the work of every single one of them more important than the transformation a good head of year team, with time to do the job quickly and properly, could bring to your school?

Teachers are good at change, if a little resistant at first. I remember when it was sacrosanct that you had to be a qualified teacher to run exams, organise cover and put up displays. Why?

P.S. I'll always be indebted to Hayley, Jill, Dynah, Tori and Emma. Thanks, everyone.

Sorting out a school which your students need and deserve

This will be a school where:

- Everyone is treated the same
- Low standards aren't tolerated
- Negativity is consistently challenged
- The time is taken to build robust, rigorous approaches to behavioural problems
- People talk about values, not rules
- Senior leaders know the children in their school and take genuine joy in their learning and successes

Sorting out advice to senior leaders

It's worth bearing in mind the following, all of which I've learned from great school leaders:

- Abide by the same values you have set for everyone
- Be intolerant sometimes
- Pick up litter
- Visit every classroom at least once a week[*]
- Ensure the default setting on your office door is 'open'
- Thank people, a lot: if you can't think of what to thank them for, you don't know well enough what they are doing
- Set up a system whereby giving a student's name to the office generates a letter of praise home
- Allow students who have done great work to be sent you and willingly interrupt meetings to welcome them in for a couple of minutes
- Realise the incredible danger in trying to run the school from your office

---

[*]This is actually a doddle: it sends out a powerful message, keeps people on their toes and means you can occasionally shut your office door without feeling guilty.

- Get to know a large cross-section of students – going on the occasional trip, sitting in on the school council and so on are great for this
- Use discipline with regret
- Remember that behaviour and learning are two sides of the same coin – one has a profound effect on the other

Sorting out the things naughty students love

The following can actually fan the flames!

- Having the wonderful validation of seeing their name written in large letters on the board

- Getting detentions which they know they will never actually serve. Either the system is so full of holes they simply won't have to bother or a kind member of the pastoral team will completely undermine the teacher by cancelling it, believing they'll suddenly stop misbehaving as a result of this wonderful kindness (which is unlikely)

- Being sent out of lessons. This is great: you can make the teacher look ridiculous by waving through the window (or worse!), wander off and make other teachers also look ridiculous, and make sure as many other students as possible see how special and different you are by not having to be in lessons, like them

Conclusion

Can you improve behaviour in your school?   Yes

Should you improve behaviour in your school?   Yes

These things can be done. Every situation can be improved. You can do it.

Final bit

I look back on the last few years at Pool Business and Enterprise College and Sir John Leman High School with immense pride, both in the impact we were able to have and in the magnificent teams at both schools, in particular Paul Annear, Leighton Tellem, Alan Myers, Mike Wilson, Mike Taylor, David Castleton and Emma Burton.

In terms of behaviour, neither became the perfect school. Things still went wrong. But a lot less. The difficulties that were prevented are incalculable, as are the negative impacts each disruption would have had on lessons, teachers and children.

978-178135100-0

978-178135003-4

978-178135104-8

i www.independentthinkingpress.com